DEFINING
THE
MOMENT

DECISIONS & ACTIONS THAT
IMPACT YOUR LIFE

EMMANUEL ATOE

WESTBOW
PRESS®
A DIVISION OF THOMAS NELSON
& ZONDERVAN

WestBow Press books may be ordered through booksellers or by contacting:

WestBow Press
A Division of Thomas Nelson & Zondervan
1663 Liberty Drive
Bloomington, IN 47403
www.westbowpress.com
844-714-3454

Cover Design by Signs Madueke

ISBN: 978-1-6642-5180-9 (sc)
ISBN: 978-1-6642-5181-6 (e)

Print information available on the last page.

WestBow Press rev. date: 3/17/2022

DEDICATION

This book is dedicated to my family.

A special thanks goes to Mountain of Fire and Miracle Ministry Assistant General Overseer Abiodun Ladejola

Thank you for believing in me and inspiring me to success. Your kindness, gentleness, love, and the presence of God makes my life full of joy. The LORD blesses you and keep you; The LORD makes His face shine upon you and be gracious to you; The LORD lifts up His countenance upon you and give you peace, in Jesus' Name. Amen.

Always be full of joy in the Lord. I say it again - rejoice!

INTRODUCTION

Listen to my prayer, O God, do not ignore my plea; hear me and answer me. My thoughts trouble me and I am distraught because of what my enemy is saying, because of the threats of the wicked; for they bring down suffering on me and assail me in their anger. My heart is in anguish within.

Define the moment or the moment will define you. There is a point at which the essential nature or character of a person, group, event, etc., is revealed or identified. There are moments in everyone's life that can be considered "defining moments". There are times, powerful situations and of course significant moments which greatly change the course of their future. This could be an event that happened to a person. This defining moment ultimately impacts their identity. I am convinced that when we take the time to meditate and focus on these important moments, everyone would agree that such events can impact a person positively to live a better life.

As for me, I call to God, and the Lord saves me. Evening, morning, and noon I cry out in distress, and he hears my voice. He rescues me unharmed from the battle waged against me, even though many oppose me.

CONTENTS

ONE
VISUALIZE YOUR FUTURE!

THERE IS A strong drive-in every person embedded within their subconscious motivating them to go after successful achievement in life. Dreams and vision are intricately linked.

> "Where there is no revelation, people cast off restraint;
> but blessed is the one who heeds wisdom's instruction."

— PROVERBS 29:18

The dream you have will give you the motivation and the urge, which will prevent you from never giving up or discouraged on the pathway to success. That moment you stood your ground in the face of challenges and trial and deciding, "Give up is not an option. Give it another try, don't throw in the towel" – could be a defining moment for you.

Any person who desires to be successful must be a good dreamer. God has given everyone from birth the ability to dream. A hopefully believing within their inner mind what they would eventually achieve before it happened. The ability of living within their subconscious, the good dreams until it eventually became a reality in the natural. Most successful men and women had inner image of what they eventually achieved prior to their greatness. They dreamt about achieving that success from childhood, winning medals, or doing a particular job. That calling has always been in their spirit or subconscious mind to achieve that success and bless mankind.

It is a gift we all have right from infants to dream and visualize our future. We all have the ability to visualize and practice behind the scenes what we would eventually do publicly. The fact is that not everyone succeeds in realizing their good dreams. Some live in disappoint and regrets due to failure to achieve their desired good dreams. Some visualize in their inner eye and are able to achieve and accomplish their goals in the natural while others have stopped completely to have dream. They feed on bad dreams with no hope and motivation for a good future.

Some people are highly motivated and know how to get what they wanted in life, while some people at a certain stage, fail to have dreams and refused to have goals, and stop applying it to their situation. They fail to meditate on God's wisdom and precepts. They do not fix their eyes on God's ways that are always better and higher. In the midst of our daily life, we must endeavour to seek God in silence and prayer. Successful men and women in the scriptures have learnt from God the truth of success secrets which most successful people also practice today. This is one of the secrets that has made them to successfully live their good dreams.

Meditation was not invented by mankind but by the almighty wisdom of God. This powerful art of visualizing their future. Visualization is not being idle, but simply seeing the invisible through your mind-eye, seeing your future with the eye of faith. What other people think or imagine about you has absolutely no impact on you but your own ability to see what no one else notices or imagined about you and your future. It is important that we think deeply and reflect on what we think, believe and our actions. In your mind's eye you must be able to imagine and see a successful and brilliant achievement concerning your future. This is renewing your mind with faith filled wisdom because most successful individual are success inside minded because they see themselves successful before they achieve success in real life.

God is doing behind the seen a new thing in your life. God's word for you is found in Prophet Isaiah.

"Forget the former things; do not dwell on the past. See,
I am doing a new thing! Now it springs up; do you not
perceive it.? I am making a way in the wilderness and
streams in the wasteland."

— ISAIAH 43:18-19

Blessed are all those who trust the Lord. Those who have chosen
to live a lifestyle trusting God's best are truly blessed. In difficulties,
trials, and good times. God is always drawing our attention to a path
that is always open and on which we can walk daily, secured of His
everlasting presence. There is no person in this world that can reach
his [her] destiny without opposition, but great things God has prepared
for your future is greater than challenges confronting you or that you
have faced in your past. The Lord does not simply bring you out of the
hardship but actually brings you out better than you were before the
crisis. That is, you come out better than you were before the challenges
the adversary thought could bring down.

"For my thoughts are not your thoughts, neither are
your ways my ways," declares the LORD. As the heavens
are higher than the earth, so are my ways higher than
your ways and my thoughts than your thoughts."

— ISAIAH 55:8-9

The infinite thoughts of the almighty God are far greater than
what our limited minds can understand. The ways of the living God
are awesome, vast and although they do not always make sense to us,
but we can rest assured in the truth that our God is always good, all
His works and everything about Him is exceptionally good. The Lord
is good and ready to forgive. God is abundant in lovingkindness to all
who call upon Him. The Lord is good to all, and His mercies are over
all His works.

So, God is always good, and therefore we should expect the
manifestation of His goodness in our lives. The awesome news is that
thanks to God, Jesus' birth, life, death, resurrection, and ascension

revealed God's loving kindness and most especially opened it up to people on the earth. This goodness is no longer only opened to a privilege chosen nation, but now it is for everyone. John 3:16 (NIV), *"For God so loved the world that he gave his one and only Son, that whoever believes in him shall not perish but have eternal life."* The Lord Jesus has made it possible for all to come to the throne of grace, equal and united before the creator of Heaven and Earth. The earth is the Lord's, and everything in it, the world, and all who live in it.

> "The earth is the Lord's, and everything in it, the world, and all who live in it; for he founded it on the seas and established it on the waters."

> — PSALM 24:1-2

We can fully trust God even when we don't completely understand. We must have faith in His Word even when it seems difficult, humanly impossible, and maybe cruel. We become frustrated when we try to comprehend God's ways with our limited understanding.

> "For my thoughts are not your thoughts, neither are your ways my ways, declares the LORD. As the heavens are higher than the earth, so are my ways higher than your ways and my thoughts than your thoughts."

> — ISAIAH 55:8-9

God's ways are higher than those of mankind, and our minds cannot always comprehend His actions because they do not always make sense to us. When the forces of darkness prosper and righteous people are confronted with serious challenges people question God's ways and love. However. We must understand and know fully well in our heart that the Lord is always good, loving and kind to us.

"For the Lord is always good. He is always loving and kind, and his faithfulness goes on and on to each succeeding generation."

— PSALM 100:5

Taking a very deep reflection of our life and a look at the lives of many of the people we know that have made it successfully in life, it will occur to us that there are a few key moments that made them what they are now. Can we call these events and the consequent actions they took their defining moments? You may be wondering; we all have different event and action in our lives that impacted our lives forever. So, can we look to that as individual's defining moments? What you see, "Yourself image" and your vision about your life is very important in the event of challenges and crisis.

"The eye is the lamp of the body. If your eyes are healthy, your whole body will be full of light. But if your eyes are unhealthy your whole body will be full of darkness. If then the light within you is darkness, how great is that darkness!"

— MATTHEW 6:22-23

That is why we must look on to the direction of the Holy Spirit, whatever the situation because God is good to all and He will direct our ways, if we lean on Him for guidance and direction.

"The Lord is good to all; he has compassion on all he has made.

— PSALM 145:9

We are not to judge our worth and ability to approach God based upon our birth, family lineage, self-righteousness, good work, and any ritual based sacrifices. We approach God in the name of our Lord Jesus, by trusting His love, mercy, and taking refuge in Him because He care for us exceedingly abundantly. In all circumstances, we are invited to taste and see that the Lord is good.

> "Taste and see that the Lord is good; blessed is the one who takes refuge in Him."

— PSALM 34:8

All believers are one in the great Family of God by having *spiritual* ties to Abraham by means of a spiritual birth though faith in the messiah, built upon the rock Jesus Christ our Lord and Savior.

> "So, also Abraham believed God, and it was credited to him as righteousness. Understand, then, that those who have faith are children of Abraham. Scripture foresaw that God would justify the Gentiles by faith and announced the gospel in advance to Abraham: "All nations will be blessed through you." So those who rely on faith are blessed along with Abraham, the man of faith."

— GALATIANS 3:6-9

> "Moses thought that his own people would realize that God was using him to rescue them, but they did not."

— ACT 7:25

What defines us is not necessary what we go through but the power of God's love. The Holy Spirit through the revelation given to us by Deacon Stephen tells us that Moses went out to visit "his brethren." Although Moses was raised up as the son of Pharoah's daughter, his nursing mother, who by God's favour happens to be the Hebrew very woman who gave birth to him must have related to him his origin and true story.

"By faith Moses, when he became of age, refused to be called the son of Pharaoh's daughter, choosing rather to suffer affliction with the people of God than to enjoy the passing pleasures of sin, esteeming the reproach of Christ greater riches than the treasures in Egypt; for he looked to the reward. By faith he forsook Egypt, not fearing the wrath of the king; for he endured as seeing Him who is invisible."

— HEBREWS 11.24-27

So, when Moses first killed the Egyptian, he must have given thought and acknowledge his purpose in life was to try to free the people of Israel, but the timing and method was wrong, because the Almighty God always does things at exactly the right time, place, and moment. Moses assumed his fellow Israelites would realize his calling and purpose, but they did not know and obviously did not accept that God had sent him to rescue them from oppression in the land of Egypt. He mistakenly believed that his Hebrew brothers and sisters, would understand that God by his hand, was the freedom from the Egyptian bondage they cried for so long was giving to them.

They did not understand him neither did they know that God was going to use him to deliver them. The time was not right, and Moses committed murder and fled to Midian.

"In the course of time Moses grew up. Then he went to [see] his own people and watched them suffering under forced labor. He saw a Hebrew, one of his own people, being beaten by an Egyptian. He looked all around, and when he didn't see anyone, he beat the Egyptian to death and hid the body in the sand. When Moses went there the next day, he saw two Hebrew men fighting. He asked the one who started the fight, Why are you beating another Hebrew? The man asked, Who made you our ruler and judge? Are you going to kill me as you killed the Egyptian? Then Moses was afraid and thought that everyone knew what he had done. When Pharaoh heard what Moses had done, he tried to have him killed. But Moses fled from Pharaoh and settled in the land of Midian."

— EXODUS 2:11.15

Moses fled and became a dweller in the land of Midian, married Zipporah and they had two sons.

"Then, at this saying, Moses fled and became a dweller in the land of Midian, where he had two sons. And when forty years had passed, an Angel of the Lord appeared to him in a flame of fire in a bush, in the wilderness of Mount Sinai. When Moses saw it, he marvelled at the sight; and as he drew near to observe, the voice of the Lord came to him, saying, 'I am the God of your fathers - the God of Abraham, the God of Isaac, and the God of Jacob. And Moses trembled and dared not look. Then the Lord said to him, Take your sandals off your feet, for the place where you stand is holy ground. I have surely seen the oppression of My people who are in Egypt; I have heard their groaning and have come down to deliver them. And now come, I will send you to Egypt. This Moses whom they rejected, saying, 'Who made you a ruler and a judge?' is the one God sent to be a ruler and a deliverer by the hand of the Angel who appeared to him in the bush."

— ACTS 7.29-35

It must have seemed that Moses had missed his destiny and got out of God's plan and purpose. However, after forty years had passed, an Angel of the Lord appeared to him in a flame of fire in a bush, in the wilderness of Mount Sinai. This Moses whom they rejected, saying, 'Who made you a ruler and a judge?' is the one God sent to be a ruler and a deliverer by the hand of the Angel who appeared to him in the bush" Acts 7.29-35 (NKJV). What defines Moses was not necessary what he went through at the first intervention in the affair of the people of Israel but the awesome power of God's love because Romans 11:29 (NIV) says *"for God's gifts and his call are irrevocable."* So, with Moses, in his "first calling" what seems like a defeat and a failed destiny the almighty God, in His great and infinite love and favour needed to prepare Moses for his purpose by spending forty years in the wilderness and it also appears that the Israelites needed time to be prepared for his leadership. What defines Moses was not necessary the situations or circumstances but God's grace and his response or action to the exceedingly richness of God love and favour.

Moses and the Burning Bush

"Now Moses was tending the flock of Jethro his father-in-law, the priest of Midian, and he led the flock to the far side of the wilderness and came to Horeb, the mountain of God. There the angel of the LORD appeared to him in flames of fire from within a bush. Moses saw that though the bush was on fire it did not burn up. So, Moses thought, I will go over and see this strange sight - why the bush does not burn up. When the LORD saw that he had gone over to look, God called to him from within the bush, Moses! Moses! And Moses said, Here I am. Do not come any closer," God said. Take off your sandals, for the place where you are standing is holy ground. Then he said, "I am the God of your father, the God of Abraham, the God of Isaac and the God of Jacob. At this, Moses hid his face, because he was afraid to look at God. The LORD said, I have indeed seen the misery of my people in Egypt. I have heard them crying out because of their slave drivers, and I am concerned about their suffering. So, I have come down to rescue them from the hand of the Egyptians and to bring them up out of that land into a good and spacious land, a land flowing with milk and honey - the home of the Canaanites, Hittites, Amorites, Perizzites, Hivites and Jebusites. And now the cry of the Israelites has reached me, and I have seen the way the Egyptians are oppressing them. So now, go. I am sending you to Pharaoh to bring my people the Israelites out of Egypt. But Moses said to God, "Who am I that I should go to Pharaoh and bring the Israelites out of Egypt? And God said, "I will be with you. And this will be the sign to you that it is I who have sent you: When you have brought the people out of Egypt, you will worship God on this mountain. Moses said to God, "Suppose I go to the Israelites and say to them, 'The God of your fathers has sent me to you,' and they ask me, 'What is his name?' Then what shall I tell them? God said to Moses, "I AM WHO I AM. This is what you are to say to the Israelites: 'I AM has sent me to you. God also said to Moses, "Say to the Israelites, 'The LORD, the God of your fathers - the God of Abraham, the God of Isaac, and the God of Jacob – has sent me to you. This is my name forever, the name you shall call me from generation to generation. Go, assemble the elders of Israel, and say to them, The LORD, the God of your fathers - the God of Abraham, Isaac and Jacob—appeared to me and said: I have watched over you and have seen what has been done to you in Egypt. And I have promised to bring you up out of your misery in Egypt into the land of the Canaanites, Hittites, Amorites, Perizzites, Hivites and Jebusites - a land flowing with milk and honey. The elders of Israel will listen to you. Then you and the elders are to go to the king of Egypt and say to him, 'The LORD, the God of the Hebrews, has met with us. Let us take a three-day journey into the wilderness to offer sacrifices to the LORD our God. But I know that the king of Egypt will not let you go unless a mighty hand compels him. So, I will stretch out my hand and strike the Egyptians with all the wonders that I will perform among them. After that, he will let you go. And I will make the Egyptians favourably disposed toward this people, so that when you leave you will not go empty-handed. Every woman is to ask her neighbour and any woman living in her house for articles of silver and gold and for clothing, which you will put on your sons and daughters. And so, you will plunder the Egyptians."

— EXODUS 3:1

The birth of Moses was supernatural and the Lord God in supernatural power also appeared to him in the fire. Moses was drawn by the supernatural power of God to the amazing sight of the fiery bush that wasn't being consumed. The truth of the matter is that he was drawn closer to God.

"Come near to God and he will come near to you. Wash your hands, you sinners, and purify your hearts, you double-minded."

— JAMES 4:8

The sign and the wonder were what attracted Moses to the bush that was burning but not consuming and to be re-directed to walk successfully in the path of his destiny. Moses must have thought how strange the sight of a bush that was burning supernaturally, not aware it was the turning point of his life. This defining moment was about to move him to his destiny in God. Likewise, there is a defining moment in the life of a person when drawn closer to God by His grace, mercy, and love, through the supernatural power of the Holy Spirit to begin to direct the individual into God's purpose and plan for his [her] life. The destiny of Moses was so enormous that it would impact all generations, because God used him to liberate the children of God to the next phase of the eternal plan of God's great salvation. People are always drawn irresistibly to the supernatural and it is in this arena we can discover our destiny in God.

The defining moment of Moses' life was the famous second calling of an encounter with God at the burning bush. Those events are a demonstration of God's love and grace to forgive Moses' failure to fulfil successfully the first calling., trying to deliver the people of Israel by his own power and effort., and failing woefully, he fled in fear to a life of exile. Instead of allowing God's timing and method, Moses did it his way and this defining moment seems that he was out of God's plan and purpose for his life, but God's love and grace means He was not done with Moses. Romans 11:29 (NIV) says, "for God's gifts and his call are irrevocable."

Moses' life reflects our own life, relating to the grace and mercy of our Lord Jesus Christ. The heeding of God's call by Moses through the Word of God given to him is a demonstration of the working of God's gift of salvation to the Jews, and eventually to the entire world through the living Word, our Lord and Saviour Jesus Christ. Believers, how many times have we failed to heed the call to accept the gift of salvation until we eventually surrender all to God's love and grace. Almighty God is all knowing, and Jesus came at the right time, after He had prepared everything in the world, so also is the defining moment of our salvation.

> "But when the set time had fully come, God sent his
> Son, born of a woman, born under the law."

— GALATIANS 4.4

God knows everything about us, and that includes the number of our hair and our names. This knowledge about us was before we were born. Jeremiah 1:5 (NIV), "Before I formed you in the womb I knew you, before you were born, I set you apart; I appointed you as a prophet to the nations." God knew Moses before he was born, and this is evident in the supernatural circumstances of his birth.

> "When the Lord saw that he had gone over to look, God
> called to him from within the bush, "Moses! Moses!"

— EXODUS 3:4

God called him by his name and whenever we draw near to God, our names are called with love.

> "Forget the former things; do not dwell on the past. See, I am doing a new thing! Now it springs up; do you not perceive it? I am making a way in the wilderness and streams in the wasteland."

— ISAIAH 43:18-19

God wants us to draw near to him so that He can make Himself real in our lives. Just as God called *"Moses! Moses! Jesus is calling you with everlasting love. I trust you will answer the call and just like* Moses did, you will say, "Here I am." Your response to this call and not your past could be your defining moment. The past does not define your future and it does not define who you are and certainly it does not define what you will be in the future. The way to the Father is through The Cross of our Lord Jesus Christ. The precious blood of Jesus has the power to clean us from all filthiness of the past and make us righteous in the sight of God.

> "Let us draw near to God with a sincere heart and with the full assurance that faith brings, having our hearts sprinkled to cleanse us from a guilty conscience and having our bodies washed with pure water."

— HEBREW 10:22

The blood of Jesus will purge us, and the Word of God will clean us so that we can experience the wonderful presence of God's grace and love.

The light of God's presence through the written Word will expel every form of darkness in our lives, until we become spotless or without blemishes. Moses took off his shoes and we are called to embrace the grace gift of God that takes away completely the sin of the past so that we can follow the ways of God. Taking off one's shoes could be an expression of giving yourself completely without any interference or intermediary to a place, course, plan, or purpose. Jesus washes His disciples' feet and after said:

> "You call me 'Teacher' and 'Lord,' and rightly so, for that is what I am. Now that I, your Lord and Teacher, have washed your feet, you also should wash one another's feet. I have set you an example that you should do as I have done for you. Very truly I tell you, no servant is greater than his master, nor is a messenger greater than the one who sent him. Now that you know these things, you will be blessed if you do them."
>
> — JOHN 13:13-17

God introduces Himself to Moses who hid his face for conviction of sin and fear of looking at God, but quickly acknowledged his sinful past. God of mercy called him, just like He does with us when we acknowledge our sin nature and look unto Jesus finished work by His death, resurrection and sitting at the right hand of God. After Moses has taken off his shoes God revealed His great plan to deliver the people from bondage and the important role Moses has to play, in the destiny of Israel. God has great promises and plan for us that has never changed, nor will it ever change, but with faith we must be strong, courageous and stand strong and trust God.

TWO

DESIRE

"Take delight in the LORD, and he will give you the desires of your heart."

— PSALM 37:4

THOUGH WE MAY not have the spectacular burning supernatural bush to define our moment, I sincerely believe that we all have without doubt our defining moments. The dictionary definition of a defining moment is an event that influences or changes all subsequent related occurrences. It is an important moment that enables us to identify what is our calling and the person we are in our lives. They are moments triggered by particular events that change our way of thinking and behaviour. They are the steppingstones to personal growth and self-development. There are different cases, while some people may have defining moments that change the course of their lives for the good, others fail to recover from the result or consequent of their action. You may be asking these questions, what are my defining moments or when is my defining moment going to show up? The questions you ask will determine your destiny. Questions will enable you to deal with the problem of ignorance. Whatever your destination or position in life, asking questions will enable you obtain and be properly guided. Fools decline and despise questions to embrace ignorance. The secret of life is found in questions.

> "Though you grind a fool in a mortar, grinding them like grain with a pestle, you will not remove their folly from them"

— PROVERBS 27:22

Life is full of questions. Questions about the past, present and future. Any person who is interested in success in life must ask questions about his [or her] past, present, and future. There is no personal development for a person who is not able to locate one or several defining moments in their past. The unfortunate thing is that a vast majority of people go through life without the awareness of the power of the defining moment. Sadly, the majority of people are actually not unaware there are defining moments. They desire the best in life but fail to identify for themselves, how to figure life defining moment. The secret of life is found in moments of crisis that builds a strong character inner strength, which as a life-changing role is very vital and can be powerfully brought forth outwardly when needed, to overcome future challenges. These are moments that allow you to know who you are and what you are truly made of, in terms of character. This will reveal to you your true character, i.e., your inner strength. It gives the inner push when you really desire something that is really important to you, the internal motivation will give you the extra push and effort. to succeed. This strong desire comes with hope and strength looking always for the right possibilities and good opportunities in the journey of life, even in the mist of adversities. God has promised to be with us and that He will never leave us nor forsake us. That's a very powerful promise when you have a strong desire. God says to us today what He told Moses,

> "God said to Moses, I AM WHO I AM. This is what you are to say to the Israelites: 'I AM has sent me to you.'"

— EXODUS 3:14

What an incredibly powerful statement. The all-powerful One, who was with Moses, is also with you, so your past does not define your life, you can desire the best for your future. God gives us His Words and promises over the entire situation. God gave Moses a complete picture and full details of the very words to speak and Pharoah's exact response, and how Israel would regain back all their wealth before they depart from the land of Egypt. Jesus came to assist us regain our promised land and repossess what belong to us from the power of darkness, who is currently occupying that land that belong to some people. This does not mean promising Christians a bed of roses, our desire can be attained knowing there will always be a good fight of faith, to take over and enjoy the good promises Jesus Christ must be the anchor of our faith, because just as the elders did not accepted Moses, your desire may not be shared by others, or some people may not believe in you. The desire may be great, but you cannot take everyone aboard until they are convinced about the purpose of your desire and the added value to their lives. Moses and the elders went to Pharoah and informed him exactly God's Words, so also you must confront the past with the Word of God to accomplish your God given desire. The Word of God tells us exactly through His promises what He will do for us to achieve the desire of our heart. God always gives another chance when we fail to do the right thing. When we humble ourselves in submission to God's will, we are given chances to choose the right path in the issues of life. God promises grace, guidance, and a wealth transfer to those who trust Him. God restored the wealth to the people of Israel after 400 years of hard labour. The people of Israel departed from the promised land healthy, wealthy, and victorious over the enemy of their progress. God wants us to accomplish our heart desire healthy, wealthy, and victorious in all areas of life.

> "Dear friend, I pray that you may enjoy good health and that all may go well with you, even as your soul is getting along well."
>
> — 3 JOHN 2

What defines you is not necessary the situations or circumstances but God's grace and your response or action to the exceedingly richness of God love and favour. Our first love and desire should be Jesus and to please God. Believers are called to place their hope in God, who promises, never fail. So, our faith and trust, therefore, should be in Jesus alone. Keep your lives free from the love of money and be content with what you have, because God has said, "*Never will I leave you; never will I forsake you.*" We should look unto the giver with trust and faith and not to the gift. Hebrews 13:5 (NIV), restates the promise of God's eternal presence with believers. The eternal promise of God that He will never leave or forsake believers is not only comforting, but also provides courage to followers of Christ. The children of God can live without fear, because the Lord who is good and faithful will never leave or forsake them.

However, for us to accomplish the desire of our heart, we must enter God's Holy realm by removing our old ways. The presence, plan and purpose of God will release an internal explosion into our life, that will propel us into success and greatness by faith. When our desire is in-line with God's desire for us, no human being alive can determine the magnitude of what would happen if and when we dare to enter His Holy realm by removing our old ways. Any person that desires to walk into his [or her] destiny and leave his [or her] mark or footprint successfully on earth must have a deep relationship with the Holy Spirit, in submission allow Him to deal with the past, direct the present and surrender the future. The blessing comes when the old idols are abandoned to possess the priestly role of His grace and love. When we desire God and His ways, it will lead us out of darkness into His marvellous light. Whatever is your profession, calling or livelihood, if you are faithful you can move to the top. On that faithful day, Moses as usual went out doing his job, taking care of his own business, the sheep of Jethro his father-in-law, little did he know that it was a day that will be his define moment for life. A day he will never forget because he ends up at the very mountain of God. A defining moment of his life, he came to the place of his calling. The love and grace of God gives you the opportunity that you can have a new beginning no matter what the mess up in your life. There are stories of many people who have started out in some profession and made a failure of it because they haven't waited upon God for instruction, or direction and not exercising patience to hear the voice of God. I cannot over emphasize the importance of preparation and being well equipped for service, however just like Moses in the Egyptian schools for kingship, and all the advantages any man would like to have, undoubtedly, he failed woefully. Promotion comes from the Lord and no person can enjoy an everlasting success without the favour of the almighty God who gives wisdom and guidance.

Moses first and second experiences in Egypt were moment in time that defines his failure and success achievement. Both moment in time had a negative and positive effect on him. The first event he acted alone on his own ability and wisdom. This led to his committing murder and had to flee as a fugitive. The way he acted led him from kingship to fugitive in exile. The second event he acted empowered, directed, and full of God's wisdom. This led to his leading six million people as a "god" to Pharoah out of the Land of Egypt to the Promise Land. The way he acted led him from fugitive to one of the greatest men ever lived on earth. The first moment in Egypt was less dramatic, than the second moment but they both had a meaningful impact on him and ultimately on the whole world.

What defines Moses was not necessary the situations or circumstances but God's grace and his response or action to the exceedingly richness of God love and favour. With the favour and power to change you will understand your past more clearly, because it will have impactful moments in your life.

> "that the sharing of your faith may become effective by the acknowledgment of every good thing which is in you in Christ Jesus."
>
> — PHILEMON 1:6

We must realize that people with past successes have the ability to connect to their internal strengths and therefore move forward in future endeavours with greater confidence. Therefore, a positive memory accompanied by strong faith is recommended for those who desire to be successful in life projects. The fact that every defining moment in life might not be positive, the grace and power to have a positive vision or dream in important events or situations of the past is essential to visualize a successful future. God does not define you by your past mistakes, failure and bad decision, There is always a new beginning, no matter how far you must have failed. God can use our mistakes, failures, wrong decisions when we receive His forgiveness, mercy, grace, and wisdom.

PETER DENIES JESUS

"Then they seized him and led him away, bringing him into the high priest's house, and Peter was following at a distance. And when they had kindled a fire in the middle of the courtyard and sat down together, Peter sat down among them. Then a servant girl, seeing him as he sat in the light and looking closely at him, said, "This man also was with him." But he denied it, saying, "Woman, I do not know him." And a little later someone else saw him and said, "You also are one of them." But Peter said, "Man, I am not." And after an interval of about an hour still another insisted, saying, "Certainly this man also was with him, for he too is a Galilean." But Peter said, "Man, I do not know what you are talking about." And immediately, while he was still speaking, the rooster crowed. And the Lord turned and looked at Peter. And Peter remembered the saying of the Lord, how he had said to him, "Before the rooster crows today, you will deny me three times." And he went out and wept bitterly."

— LUKE 22:54-62

We are aware of the fact that in the life of any person, when a repetition becomes consistent, the person creates patterns that become habits, which then become personality traits, and these define who the person is at that point in time. Jesus did not define Peter by his past mistakes, failure, and repeated denials. What defines Peter was not necessary the situations or circumstances but God's grace and his response or action to the exceedingly richness of God love and favour.

When the Sabbath was past, Mary Magdalene, Mary the mother of James, and Salome bought spices, so that they might go and anoint him. And very early on the first day of the week, when the sun had risen, they went to the tomb. And they were saying to one another, "Who will roll away the stone for us from the entrance of the tomb?" And looking up, they saw that the stone had been rolled back - it was very large. And entering the tomb, they saw a young man sitting on the right side, dressed in a white robe, and they were alarmed. And he said to them, "Do not be alarmed. You seek Jesus of Nazareth, who was crucified. He has risen; he is not here. See the place where they laid him. But go, tell his disciples and Peter that he is going before you to Galilee. There you will see him, just as he told you."

— MARK 16:7

The love and grace of God gave Peter the opportunity to have a new beginning not withstanding his mess up by denying Jesus during crucifixion. No believer will ever have that type of defining moment, but we all have defining moments more frequently, less dramatic with minor impact, that we fail to recognize because we remember only those that are dramatic and have a major impact in our lives. However, the defining moments whether less dramatic with minor impact or more dramatic with major impact, there is always a new beginning no matter how far a person may have gone from the path of his or her destiny. So, your defining moment could be a point in life when decision meets action.

We all have defining moments that are created by minor and major actions and these moments, to some extent could determine who we are today. The action of Peter at the moment he was recognized as one of Jesus disciples and his immediate response leaves the greatest impression on his life, and although he was not aware of the impact when it actually happened. The fact that it happened three times makes it even more dramatic and had great impact in his life. Peter did not plan to lie and to be dishonest. His desire was to demonstrate his love, trust, integrity, unfailing loyalty to Jesus, but in a moment of weakness and probably fear for his life, he compromises his integrity and lied. Likewise, our strong desire and some important decisions we make could give birth to produce consequences that could give shape to our behaviour, determine our integrity, and ultimately control our destiny. The divine intervention of God's love and grace gave Peter a new beginning. Peters' past mistakes did not define his future to serve Christ. It did not define who he became and what he did for the kingdom of God. He still fulfilled his divine destiny successfully. The truth is defining moments in Peters life enabled him to refine his passions, faith, and love of Jesus to live purposeful, and lead a successful Christian life. Likewise in our lives defining moments could enable us to refine our passions, desire, goals and plans to live purposeful, and have successful lives.

The event which are moments in our lives will influence or change all subsequent related occurrences because the decisions we make or actions we take have consequences. A moment that reveals the true character of a person, as evident in the lives of the men and women of faith in the Holy Bible, who encountered their own defining moments and chose to stand-up for what they believe, what was right against opposition and difficult choice. The courageous men and women God used to reveal His plan, purpose and unveils the future despite their past mistakes, failure, and weakness. God wants to give you the desire of your heart even in the event of past mistakes and errors.

> "May He give you the desire of your heart and make all your plans succeed."

— PSALM 20:4

According to scripture, God wants to fulfill His plans and purposes in each of our lives when we submit in humility. The Holy Spirit wants to impact our lives, take our weakness, failures, and defeats as we respond to the life-changing truths and power revealed through the anointed Word of God.

> "But God chose the foolish things of the world to shame the wise; God chose the weak things of the world to shame the strong."

— 1 CORINTHIANS 1:27

There are powerful and awesome testimonies in the lives of men and women who had divine encounter with God in a defining moment and answered the unique supreme call on their lives.

> "Concerning this salvation, the prophets, who spoke of the grace that was to come to you, searched intently and with the greatest care, trying to find out the time and circumstances to which the Spirit of Christ in them was pointing when he predicted the sufferings of the Messiah and the glories that would follow. It was revealed to them that they were not serving themselves but you, when they spoke of the things that have now been told you by those who have preached the gospel to you by the Holy Spirit sent from heaven. Even angels long to look into these things."

— 1 PETER 1:10-12

This power inspires us to hunger and desire to seek daily the presence of God, to have an encounter with the Lord Jesus through the anointing of the Holy Spirit. The desire for a divine visitation is the gate way for empowerment into the realm of signs, wonders and miracle enabling us to fulfil a greater measure of our divine destiny.

THREE

DIRECTION

IS DIRECTION POSSIBLE from a defining moment? A defining moment is any time in your life in which a choice that you make or an incident that happens causes something in your life to change. It is something that from that particular moment on defines some aspect of your life. In the journey of life, we all have various moments. Every day we have defining moments that are created by action. Based on individual perspective, it is possible for people to have many defining moments throughout their lifetimes. Defining moments are endless and available for personal interpretation. Though there are no particular limits, but when they occur, each moment will undoubtedly have a huge impact on the person's life. Actually, we face defining moments more often that we realize and some of these moments can be marriage, childbirth, separations, divorce, receiving an award, graduation, becoming a Christian (Salvation or born-again), major storm or trials, tribulation, important breakthroughs and victories over long-term issues or problems.

The people who are interested in personal development are often more likely to be able to carefully locate one or several defining moment in their past. Most people are not careful about these moments and could go through life without having knowledge or any awareness of the awesome power of the defining moment in their lives. These people who are not aware that there are defining moments, cannot recognize a point in their lives when decision meets action. They failed to realize how important these moments are to them in the journey of life. The main reason they fail to recognize them for what they are, could be simply because they sometimes occur quickly and frequently. So, essential to know that anyone who wants direction for a successful life should develop good habits because they are bound to create personality traits, that could eventually define the person they become in the near future. Although our various actions or lack of actions will ultimately give direction or determine who we are to a large extent, more than we realise the decision not to do something has a greatest impression on our lives.

If we trust the direction of our heart, and follow-up the good decision with an action diligently, we will get the benefits. When we set goals and then take the necessary action of planning to execute them properly, we will achieve the desire of our heart. The defining moments to these points are those of a person who will not only dream, but who will also follow through, take the necessary positive action, and achieve success. The direction is goals are life changers, but you must take the required actions or else you will not be a success. Some people define themselves or allow other people to define them as failures. You are not a failure until you decide to quite, don't be a quitter. Do not give up and do not allow other people's opinion, situation, circumstances, or the mistakes to define you. Isaiah 43:19 (NIV), "Behold, I will do a new thing; now it shall spring forth; shall ye not know it? I will even make a way in the wilderness, and rivers in the desert."

There is always a possibility for new opportunities that will come to define your life. So be prepared to change direction when the right opportunities come your way and be prepared to take the essential actions. The direction you take will lead to an action which will determine the success or failure to attain your set goals. The direction comes from the decisions you make which on the long-term will determine your action, integrity, and may subsequently control your destiny. The moment you make the decision to act, but you failed to do something beware that is essential, this will certainly have a strong impact in your life.

Direction comes from decisions and actions that impact the life of a person. Most people have divine moments like the men and women in the scriptures who had life-altering moments that turned their dreams into a life of success. They are living or enjoying the reality of their desired dreams, What defines these people's lives is not necessary the situations or circumstances but God's grace and their response or action to the exceedingly richness of God love and favour. These are particular moments that have changed the lives of men and women more relevantly directing them to capture their destiny. These people depending on the moment, and how they reacted to these decisions have changed their lives.

A DIVINE ENCOUNTER THAT CHANGED THE LIFE OF APOSTLE PAUL IN ACTS 9

The amazing defining moment in the life of Apostle Paul, is his conversion to a devout Christian, from a life of a strong pharisee Jew. Paul in possession of a letter of authority to persecute, arrest and jail those who believe in Jesus Christ had a divine encounter with the Lord Jesus on the road of Damascus. He immediately went about boldly spreading the Gospel without compromise and against violent opposition, as recorded in three instances in the book of Acts of the Apostles. Once again what defines Apostle Paul was not necessary the situations or circumstances but God's grace and his response or action to the exceedingly richness of God's love and favour.

Saul's Conversion

"Meanwhile, Saul was still breathing out murderous threats against the Lord's disciples. He went to the high priest and asked him for letters to the synagogues in Damascus, so that if he found any there who belonged to the Way, whether men or women, he might take them as prisoners to Jerusalem. As he neared Damascus on his journey, suddenly a light from heaven flashed around him. He fell to the ground and heard a voice say to him, "Saul, Saul, why do you persecute me?" "Who are you, Lord?" Saul asked. "I am Jesus, whom you are persecuting," he replied. Now get up and go into the city, and you will be told what you must do." The men traveling with Saul stood there speechless; they heard the sound but did not see anyone. Saul got up from the ground, but when he opened his eyes, he could see nothing. So, they led him by the hand into Damascus. For three days he was blind and did not eat or drink anything. In Damascus there was a disciple named Ananias. The Lord called to him in a vision, "Ananias!" "Yes, Lord," he answered. The Lord told him, "Go to the house of Judas on Straight Street and ask for a man from Tarsus named Saul, for he is praying. In a vision he has seen a man named Ananias come and place his hands on him to restore his sight." "Lord," Ananias answered, "I have heard many reports about this man and all the harm he has done to your holy people in Jerusalem. And he has come here with authority from the chief priests to arrest all who call on your name." But the Lord said to Ananias, "Go! This man is my chosen instrument to proclaim my name to the Gentiles and their kings and to the people of Israel. I will show him how much he must suffer for my name. Then Ananias went to the house and entered it. Placing his hands on Saul, he said, "Brother Saul, the Lord - Jesus, who appeared to you on the road as you were coming here - has sent me so that you may see again and be filled with the Holy Spirit." Immediately, something like scales fell from Saul's eyes, and he could see again. He got up and was baptized, and after taking some food, he regained his strength.

— ACTS *9:1-22*

SAUL IN DAMASCUS AND JERUSALEM

Saul spent several days with the disciples in Damascus. At once he began to preach in the synagogues that Jesus is the Son of God. All those who heard him were astonished and asked, "Isn't he the man who raised havoc in Jerusalem among those who call on this name? And hasn't he come here to take them as prisoners to the chief priests?" Yet Saul grew more and more powerful and baffled the Jews living in Damascus by proving that Jesus is the Messiah.

In the above Saul's he was on a mission of persecuting Christians in Jerusalem and Judea, and for this purpose he obtained permission from the high priest, and then set out for Damascus, with a zeal to find and arrest Christians who had fled his persecution. On his journey, suddenly a light from heaven flashed around him. He fell to the ground and heard a voice say to him why he was persecuting Him. The voice then told him what to do. Saul, became blind, and his companions led him to Damascus where he fasted for three days.

In Damascus there was a disciple named Ananias who *in a vision*, the Lord commanded to meet Saul and minister to him. Ananias obeyed despite his fear of Saul of Tarsus, the persecutor of Christians. Saul, whose name later became Paul, regained his sight, broke his three days fast and began his powerful and bold ministry. Ananias placed his hands on Saul, declared the Lord's message and immediately something like scales fell from his eyes, he regained his sight, he was baptized, and he took food and water. The scripture says that placing his hands on Saul, he said, "Brother Saul, the Lord – Jesus, who appeared to you on the road as you were coming here – has sent me so that you may see again and be filled with the Holy Spirit." Immediately, something like scales fell from Saul's eyes, and he could see again. He got up and was baptized, and after taking some food, he regained his strength.

In Acts 22, during his trial before the Jews, Paul spoke about his conversion. Paul returned to Jerusalem after many years of preaching Christ without compromise throughout Asia Minor and Greece. Paul was arrested because some the Jews falsely accused him of bringing a Gentile into the temple. Paul was given permission to speak for himself and he did in their native "Hebrew dialect." He reminded them that was a Jew, brought up and educated under the famous Jewish teacher Gamaliel. He spoke about his previous zeal in persecuting Christians and his mission to Damascus with a letter to arrest and persecute Christians. Paul spoke about his divine encounter regarding the bright light and Jesus Christ voice saying, "I am Jesus whom you are persecuting."

In Acts 26, Paul gave more details about this divine encounter on the road to Damascus. It happened after over one year in prison, that he had the opportunity to testify, defend himself and ministry before the Judean king Agrippa. Paul confessed before the audience about his old lifestyle of persecuting Christians and confirmed the encounter, the voice he heard informed him that "it is hard for you to kick against the goads." I heard a voice speaking to me and saying in the Hebrew language, 'Saul, Saul, why are you persecuting Me? It is hard for you to kick against the goads. Furthermore, Jesus Christ told him about his ministerial calling by God to bring the gospel to the Gentiles. Paul was jealously committed to this Heavenly Holy calling on given the message of the word of faith to the Gentiles. Just like Moses and Paul we need the favour and power of God to change because we must understand our past more clearly, because it will have impactful moments in our lives. The divine encounter was supernatural and awesome but what defines Paul was not necessary the situations or circumstances but God's grace and his response or action to the exceedingly richness of God love and favour.

FOUR
DISENGAGED

WHAT DEFINES YOU is not necessary your past victories or failures but God's grace and your response or action to the exceedingly richness of God love and favour. Samson was woken up from sleep by Delilah who informed him that the Philistines wanted to kill him and Samson thought, wrongly that he could go out as at other times before, and disengage himself, because he knew not that Jehovah had departed from him. Without the favour and power to change you must understand that your past more clearly, will have impactful moments in your life. Samson a Nazirite was one of the judges of Israel. He was one of the last judges before the passive Eli. This was clearly before the time of the kings when judges ruled over Israel. In those days there was no king in Israel. Everyone did what was right in his own *eyes*. What Moses had urged years earlier had been disregarded.

Samson's birth is miraculous, an angel foretold Samson's birth to his mother:

> "Behold, you are barren and have not borne children,
> but you shall conceive and bear a son"

> —JUDGES 13:5

A powerful warrior who defeated the Philistines but ignores the rules of his Nazarite vows. The consequences of pride, disobedience, and sinful relationships with women.

In the case of Samson his disobedience came in the form of Delilah, a Philistine woman whom he foolishly loved. The Philistines used this to their advantage and bribed her with 1,100 shekels to divulge the secret to Samson's strength so they can overcome him.

> "Sometime later, he fell in love with a woman in the Valley of Sorek whose name was Delilah. The rulers of the Philistines went to her and said, "See if you can lure him into showing you the secret of his great strength and how we can overpower him so we may tie him up and subdue him. Each one of us will give you eleven hundred shekels of silver." So, Delilah said to Samson, "Tell me the secret of your great strength and how you can be tied up and subdued."

—JUDGES 16:5-6

Delilah began to put pressure on Samson to reveal the secret to his great strength. It is not crystal clear that romantic attraction made Samson lose all sense. He continued with pride this relationship with Delilah despite her insistent enquiry into the secret of his strength. This ungodly relationship blinded him to truth of faithfulness to his ministry and obedience to God. Samson should have known that Delilah did not care much about him and his continued commitment to her is a testimony to the power of irresponsible, blind love.

He lies to her three times. Then she used the so-called "crocodile tears", sayings to Samson,

> "Then she said to him, "How can you say, 'I love you,' when your heart is not with me? You have mocked me these three times and have not told me where your great strength lies."

—JUDGES 16:15   33

Her persistent and perseverance was rewarded because after various trials and errors, she finally was able to procures the source of Samson's power and strength, his hair. Samson told Delilah his secret and immediately she gave the information to the Philistines and, after she cuts his hair, the scriptures say, "his *strength* left him."

> "Then she lulled him to sleep on her knees and called for a man and had him shave off the seven locks of his head. Then she began to torment him."
>
> — JUDGES 16:19

The consequences were that the Philistines seized him and gouged out his eyes and brought him down to Gaza and bound him with bronze fetters.

> "Then the Philistines took him and put out his eyes and brought him down to Gaza. They bound him with bronze fetters, and he became a grinder in the prison."
>
> — JUDGES 16:21

The Philistines blind the now weakened Samson and take him captive. He was humiliated and became a slave to the Philistine. When the Philistines called him out to entertain them at their temple, he cries out to the Lord, prayed for strength one last time.

> "Then Samson called to the LORD, saying, "O Lord GOD, remember me, I pray! Strengthen me, I pray, just this once, O God, that I may with one blow take vengeance on the Philistines for my two eyes!"
>
> — JUDGES 16:28

His prayer was answered and placing both hands on pillars supporting the temple, he pushes the two supporting ones apart and kills himself and thousands of Philistines in the process.

God gave Samson extraordinary and supernatural strength for His glory, but it was abused and most especially not "jealously guarded", The gift belongs to the Lord who has the power to take it away at any time or moment without notice or apologies. Samson didn't realize the consequences of his pride and disobedience. Samson was chosen before he was born to be used by God, but weakness of the flesh and deceitfulness of sin overpowered him. He outward appearance was a zealous Nazarite, while the truth was a slave to sin. The truth of the Scriptures is that there are many Delilah's in this world who will try to deceive you with fake love and persistently try to know your greatest secrets, weakness and may try to exploit it for their advantage or selfish gains.

Samson was disengaged from all supernatural power and strength from God. Seven of his hair locks are removed, detached, or shaved off. They did everything to withdraw from him power and supernatural strength. They could not stop the source of the supernatural strength. Although he was blinded and humiliated by the Philistines, but when he humbled himself in prayer and ask God for strength for his ministry and calling to defeat the enemy of Israel, God unconditional love and grace answered his request. Samson got back his strength for the last time killing more enemies than he ever had during his period of revenge and pride.

When you are feeling the necessity to disengaged because your past has been damaging. It is possible for you to wrongfully think that you are completely damaged forever. The rear mirror which you are looking to view your journey of life and yourself, can be full of fear, shame, disappointment, failures, rejections, guilt, and defeats. Someone may have spoken negatives words to you which can even make you feel like a worthless, misplaced, rejected, and abused. You may have had experiences in your past that are so terrible, shameful, disorganized, confusing, and sad, that for your life to be relevant, meaningful, valuable and to make sense of the person you are, it is essential to disengage from your past because it obstructs your self-perception and have great impact on your present and future

Samson's birth signifies him as a mythical figure, but it comes with a strong and significant warning: the mother must not contaminate her body with any alcohol, because her child will be a Nazirite i.e., dedicated to God from birth. Samson destiny was defined before birth. He was born to save the Israelites from the Philistines. His destiny, and his connection to the Philistines, is explicitly laid out by God even before he was born. The destiny of Jeremiah and John the Baptist were defined from the throne of Grace before birth. God granted Samson's mother this child to be dedicated and to save the Israelites, is similar to the granting of a child to Anna, who gave birth to Samuel as written in the scripture in the first book of Samuel. Prophet Samuel as in the case of Samson and John the Baptist was born to a previously barren woman. Samuel was dedicated from a young age to serve in the Temple of God in the house of prophet Eli.

While Samuel pursued with excellent spirit his calling and ministry, but Samson pursued with more passion his personal interests though God continued to direct him to fight the Philistines. He refused to listen to warnings and instructions in his relationship with Philistine women, most especially the disreputable Delilah, who had a contract with the Philistines to discover the secret of his strength. After three attempts to know the secret of his strength, and three times lying, Samson should have discontinued this toxic-relationship and put a stop to her prying into the secret of his strength, but he stubbornly failed to take proper action. Delilah did not love or care much about Samson, but his persistent slave commitment to her is a clear example and testimony of an irresponsible blind love.

Samson must have known that Delilah will take advantage of the secret information, but pride led to his fall to her nagging and manipulation. Her fake complaints and dissatisfaction about his love and continuous request to prove this love at the expense of his calling were lies because she did not love Samson, and her goal was to destroy him, and his ministry to fight the Philistines. She eventually succeeded in her plans and remove, detach, or shave off the seven locks of his hair. Samson did everything to disengage from his calling and supernatural strength.

His blindness to this disengagement eventually led to his demise because he was captured by the Philistines, blinded, and humiliated.

Also, in this case what defines Samson is not necessary the situations or circumstances but God's grace and his response or action to the exceedingly richness of God's love and favour. When Samson humbled himself in prayer and ask God to restore strength for his ministry and calling to defeat the enemy of Israel. The Philistines could not stop the source of his supernatural strength, because God's grace and unconditional love answered his request. God's plan and purpose for Samson is much more important and greater than everything, so despite his sin, God gave him back, supernatural strength to fight the Philistines. Samson got back his strength for the last time killing more enemies than he ever had during his period of revengeful wars and pride. But sadly, he also died in the last battle.

FIVE

DISCOURAGEMENT

DAVID'S CONFLICT WITH THE AMALEKITES

"Now it happened, when David and his men came to Ziklag, on the third day, that the Amalekites had invaded the South and Ziklag, attacked Ziklag and burned it with fire, and had taken captive the women and those who were there, from small to great; they did not kill anyone, but carried them away and went their way. So, David and his men came to the city, and there it was, burned with fire; and their wives, their sons, and their daughters had been taken captive. Then David and the people who were with him lifted up their voices and wept, until they had no more power to weep. And David's two wives, Ahinoam the Jezreelitess, and Abigail the widow of Nabal the Carmelite, had been taken captive.

Now David was greatly distressed, for the people spoke of stoning him, because the soul of all the people was [a]grieved, every man for his sons and his daughters.

But David strengthened himself in the LORD his God. Then David said to Abiathar the priest, Ahimelech's son, "Please bring the ephod here to me." And Abiathar brought the ephod to David. So, David inquired of the LORD, saying, "Shall I pursue this troop? Shall I overtake them?" And He answered him, "Pursue, for you shall surely overtake them and without fail recover all." So, David went, he and the six hundred men who were with him, and came to the Brook Besor, where those stayed who were left behind. But David pursued, he and four hundred men; for two hundred stayed behind, who were so weary that they could not cross the Brook Besor.

Then they found an Egyptian in the field and brought him to David; and they gave him bread and he ate, and they let him drink water. And they gave him a piece of a cake of figs and two clusters of raisins. So, when he had eaten, his strength came back to him; for he had eaten no bread nor drunk water for three days and three nights. Then David said to him, "To whom do you belong, and where are you from?" And he said, "I am a young man from Egypt, servant of an Amalekite; and my master left me behind, because three days ago I fell sick. We made an invasion of the southern area of the Cherethites, in the territory which belongs to Judah, and of the southern area of Caleb; and we burned Ziklag with fire." And David said to him, "Can you take me down to this troop?" So, he said, "Swear to me by God that you will neither kill me nor deliver me into the hands of my master, and I will take you down to this troop." And when he had brought him down, there they were, spread out over all the land, eating, and drinking and dancing, because of all the great spoil which they had taken from the land of the Philistines and from the land of Judah.

Then David attacked them from twilight until the evening of the next day. Not a man of them escaped, except four hundred young men who rode on camels and fled. So, David recovered all that the Amalekites had carried away, and David rescued his two wives. And nothing of theirs was lacking, either small or great, sons or daughters, spoil, or anything which they had taken from them; David recovered all. Then David took all the flocks and herds they had driven before those other livestock, and said, "This is David's spoil."

Now David came to the two hundred men who had been so weary that they could not follow David, whom they also had made to stay at the Brook Besor. So, they went out to meet David and to meet the people who were with him. And when David came near the people, he greeted them. Then all the wicked and worthless men of those who went with David answered and said, "Because they did not go with us, we will not give them any of the spoil that we have recovered, except for every man's wife and children, that they may lead them away and depart." But David said, "My brethren, you shall not do so with what the LORD has given us, who has preserved us and delivered into our hand the troop that came against us. For who will heed you in this matter? But as his part is who goes down to the battle, so shall his part be who stays by the supplies; they shall share alike." So it was, from that day forward; he made it a statute and an ordinance for Israel to this day.

— 1 SAMUEL 30:1-31

AT ZIG-LAG DAVID STRENGTHENS HIMSELF IN THE LORD

Life is a series of moments and moments are always changing, just like events, circumstances and situations. We cannot permit other people's opinion or behaviour to define us. There is no doubt that in defining moments our character is formed and develop the rugged inner strength. We share the story of King David because we find similarities in personal and professional identities in the life journey. There are challenges, trials, commitment, decision, and courses of action that could become irreversible. These are sources that truly revealed who we are and what we are made of (hidden character), something about us that we know or may not know but relevant to our growth and certainly relevant to other people perception about out true character.

Defining moments will reveal things that are hidden in our "inner man." Character is formed in actions during challenges that reveal our true identities. They expose things that are hidden in our heart. The story of King David who started out as a shepherd boy to become one of the greatest kings ever lived in Israel. He killed bears, lions and the giant goliath but also had some failures whenever he disobeyed God, failed to wait upon the Lord for direction or instruction, and most especially not exercising patience to hear the voice of God.

Ziklag was the military operation base of David for 16 months, in the war against the Amalekites. On this particular occasion David and his men were away pretending to collaborate with the army of Philistines to war against King Saul. The Amalekites cleverly took the opportunity to raid and destroy Ziklag. However, the Philistines to the satisfaction of Davide turned down his alliance to fight together with his men against King Saul army. David then decided to journey back to return to Ziklag. He and his men were completely worn out from north of Aphek to Ziklag, and when they arrived, they found Ziklag destroyed with smoke arising from the ashes. The found its inhabitants taken hostage and city burnt down. They had attacked Ziklag and burned it and had taken captive the women and all who were in it, both young and old. They killed none of them but carried them off as they went on their way. David and his men have lost everything.

> "Now it happened, when David and his men came to Ziklag, on the third day, that the Amalekites had invaded the South and Ziklag, attacked Ziklag and burned it with fire, and had taken captive the women and those who were there, from small to great; they did not kill anyone, but carried them away and went their way. So, David and his men came to the city, and there it was, burned with fire; and their wives, their sons, and their daughters had been taken captive."

— 1 SAMUEL 30:1-3

David and his warriors were exhausted and full of grief. David and his men wept aloud until they had no strength left to weep. In addition, David was greatly distressed because the men were talking of stoning him; each one was bitter in spirit because of his sons and daughters.

David's army the greatest ever did not hear from God and on this occasion his wisdom and strategy was completely wrong because he went with all the warriors to the north in alliance with the Philistine enemies, instead of keeping some of them at home to defend their families and city. It was obvious that everything was going wrong for David. David had to "strengthened himself" (NRSV) "or "encouraged himself" (KJV) in the Lord his God. The situation seems hopeless, everyone was depressed and discouraged, but Davide needed God's grace and wisdom not to react negatively to the rebellious members of his warriors.

The solution was to turn to the Lord almighty, so that he can find strength to go on the journey of life.

> I will lift up my eyes to the hill - From whence comes my help. My help comes from the LORD, Who made

heaven and earth. He will not allow your foot to be moved;

— PSALM 121: 1-3

"He who keeps you will not slumber." When David took his eyes off from the presence of God, he became discouraged, but he remembered the God who delivered him as a forest shepherd boy from the wild animal, and from the giant Goliath. The love and grace of God gave him the assurance and encouragement that he can have a new beginning no matter what the mess up in his life. David went before the Lord for restoration, to have his strength restored and his faith renewed.

Refreshing comes from the presence of the almighty God. Whatever the condition of an emotional and spiritual mess, God's power is able to restore.

> "He restores my soul; He leads me in the paths of righteousness For His name's sake. Yea, though I walk through the valley of the shadow of death, I will fear no evil; For You are with me; Your rod and Your staff, they comfort me."

— PSALMS 23:3-4

In the mist of this strong emotional and spiritual mess David look deep into his heart for guidance and the wisdom of the Lord to take the correct action. He took the decision to inquire of the Lord via the Urim and Thummim in the high priest's ephod a good solution he had taken in the past when he encountered challenges that needed important decision and requires urgent action.

> "But David strengthened himself in the LORD his God. Then David said to Abiathar the priest, Ahimelech's son, "Please bring the ephod here to me." And Abiathar brought the ephod to David. So, David inquired of the LORD, saying, "Shall I pursue this troop? Shall I overtake

them?" And He answered him, "Pursue, for you shall surely overtake them and without fail recover all."

— 1 SAMUEL 30:7-8

David encouraged by the Lord departed with his warriors to Ziklag. They journey without stop through the wilderness, trying to track down the Amalekites, searching for thing that gives them a clue of their passage. They found a fainted Egyptian, who they revived with water and food. It turns out he had been with the Amalekites until he was left for dead. This man asked David to Swear by God that he will neither kill him nor deliver him into the hands of his master. When Davide did, the Egyptian led him and his warriors to the camp of the Amalekite.

"And David said to him, "Can you take me down to this troop?" So, he said, "Swear to me by God that you will neither kill me nor deliver me into the hands of my master, and I will take you down to this troop."

— 1 SAMUEL *30:15*

In the battle the Amalekites were slaughtered except four hundred young men who rode on camels and fled, as the David's army fought them from dusk until the evening of the next day. This victory actually gave Israel peace against their Amalekites ferocious enemies for at least 300 years.

"Then David attacked them from twilight until the evening of the next day. Not a man of them escaped, except four hundred young men who rode on camels and fled. So, David recovered all that the Amalekites had carried away, and David rescued his two wives. And nothing of theirs was lacking, either small or great, sons or daughters, spoil, or anything which they had taken from them; David recovered all."

— 1 SAMUEL 30:17-20

In a daring rescue, David and his men pursued and defeated the Amalekites and recovered everything and everyone that were taken and captured, including his two wives Abigail. And Ahinoam. Once again, what defines David, as we see was not necessary the situations or circumstances but God's grace and his response or action to the exceedingly richness of God love and favour. David encouraged himself in the Lord, did not accept to compromise with the loss, did not accept anything less in his relationship with God.

Some days later, David received the news in Ziklag of Saul's death.

> "Now it came to pass after the death of Saul, when David had returned from the slaughter of the Amalekites, and David had stayed two days in Ziklag. on the third day, behold, it happened that a man came from Saul's camp with his clothes torn and dust on his head. So it was, when he came to David, that he fell to the ground and prostrated himself." "So, I stood over him and killed him, because I was sure that he could not live after he had fallen. And I took the crown that was on his head and the bracelet that was on his arm and have brought them here to my lord."

— 2 SAMUEL 1:1-2, 10

David from discouragement, rejection and apparently losing all, encouraged himself in the Lord and got back all his possession, but most especially after so many years after he was anointed as King by Samuel moved to Hebron to become the king of Judah.

SIX

DECISION

THESE ARE THE moments that have changed the course of your life. Life is full of decisions. The decision you took in the past is the life you are living today. If you don't set your priorities and take decision in life, someone else will do it for you. Other people will decide your priorities and goals with what they believe is most essential to you. That is certainly not a place to be. Do not allow other people to define you. Can you identify your most defining moment? Decision, decision, decision the anchor to a desired tomorrow. Life is full of choices and decisions. We make a lot of choices and decisions daily, but the truth is everyone at one moment or the other gets to the point of having to take essential decision with greater impact in life. The decision you take at that time will determine the outcome for good or bad. The Wisdom of God teaches us to appreciate the grace of God and to be grateful making the most of every moment, because every moment could lead to a defining moment.

Your action today to every moment will reveal your true personality and character and this could determine the person you will become tomorrow. Your action based on today's choices and decisions will influence your life tomorrow. The life that we desire tomorrow, will be built on the decisions we make today. The story of the journey of the Israelites to the promise land reveals various defining moments in their lives. Likewise, we also have various defining moments, but some are definitely more relevant than others. All defining moments are important, but some are more relevant because of their impact in the life of a person. Marah was a relevant turning point for the people of Israel in their journey to the promise Land. What makes it relevant is that they got to their own Marah as a part of God's plan for them. God led them to Marah as part of His plan for the Israelites. Everyone in the journey of life have various defining moments and in at least one of these moments they may eventually arrive at their own Marah. The situation that you thought and desired to be sweet but instead, it was bitter. There are various Marah, and it could be your relationship, family, business, and studies. It may be unexpected rejection, frustration, disrespect, and disappointment with people. This could be lack of peace although you are surrounded with many things that should make you to be joyful in life.

What are the right decisions to take at your own Marah? What actions can you take when you come to this situation that requires an urgent and important decision? What defines you is not necessary the situation or circumstance but God's grace and your response or action to the exceedingly richness of God love and favour.

> "Now to Him who is able to do exceedingly abundantly above all that we ask or think, according to the power that works in us, to Him be glory in the church by Christ Jesus to all generations, forever and ever. Amen."

— EPHESIANS 3:20-21

God is able to make the situation better no matter how bitter it looks at that moment. Don't limit the grace and power of the almighty God when you get to the defining moment of taking important decision. God is able to do anything at any time above all we think and desire. God is able to do immeasurably more than all we ask or imagine, according to his power that is at work within us. Those who lose focus on God's blessing will limit God. The limit is not God but the boundary they draw in their minds. God got angry with the Children of Israelites because of complains and murmurs when they came to the bitter water, they forgot about the previous miracle at the Red Sea that was parted, and the spontaneous praises and worship service led by Miriam after they walked through on dry ground.

God gave the success formula to Joshua, but some people fail at the defining moment of decision while others succeed. We have to first recognize that the life we want tomorrow is built on the decisions we make today. We have to recognize that the defining moment is locked up in the actions we take based on our decisions.

THE STORY OF BARTIMAEUS

Jesus Heals Blind Bartimaeus

"Now they came to Jericho. As He went out of Jericho with His disciples and a great multitude, blind Bartimaeus, the son of Timaeus, sat by the road begging. And when he heard that it was Jesus of Nazareth, he began to cry out and say, "Jesus, Son of David, have mercy on me!" Then many warned him to be quiet; but he cried out all the more, "Son of David, have mercy on me!" So, Jesus stood still and commanded him to be called. Then they called the blind man, saying to him, "Be of good cheer. Rise, He is calling you." And throwing aside his garment, he rose and came to Jesus. So, Jesus answered and said to him, "What do you want Me to do for you?" The blind man said to Him, "Rabboni, that I may receive my sight." Then Jesus said to him, "Go your way; your faith has made you well." And immediately he received his sight and followed Jesus on the road."

— MARK 10:46-56

The story reveals that what defines Bartimaeus was not necessary the situations or circumstances but God's grace and his decision or action to the exceedingly richness of God love and favour. His life after the encounter with Jesus was built on the decisions, he took on that day he met Jesus on the road of Jericho. He recognized that his defining moment is locked up in the actions he takes based on his decisions. Bartimaeus was a blind beggar who called out to Jesus for mercy and healing, as He went out from Jericho on His last journey to Jerusalem. He must have heard of Jesus and his miracles, and learning that he was passing by, hoped to recover his eyesight.

Bartimaeus had an unshaken faith demonstrated by calling Jesus the Son of God and would not be denied, although the crowd tried their best to keep him quiet. He realizes that was his moment of a lifetime. A defining moment and his action was to shout or cry out louder. His determination and loud cry halted Jesus who tells his disciples to bring the blind man over. He then cast away his garment, a lesson everyone that comes to Jesus must emulate, by cast away the garment of past failures, defeats, rejection, and the weight of sin. We must receive the miracle of salvation by faith and walk in the light.

THE STORY OF THE WOMAN WITH ISSUE OF BLOOD

The story of the woman with issue of blood for 12 years

"And a woman having an issue of blood twelve years, which had spent all her living upon physicians, neither could be healed of any, Came behind him, and touched the border of his garment: and immediately her issue of blood stanched. And Jesus said, Who touched me? When all denied, Peter and they that were with him said, Master, the multitude throng thee and press thee, and sayest thou, Who touched me? And Jesus said, Somebody hath touched me: for I perceive that virtue is gone out of me. And when the woman saw that she was not hid, she came trembling, and falling down before him, she declared unto him before all the people for what cause she had touched him, and how she was healed immediately. And he said unto her, Daughter, be of good comfort: thy faith hath made thee whole; go in peace."

— LUKE 8:43-48

The story of this woman another evidence that what defines her was not necessary the situations or circumstances but God's grace and her decision or action to the exceedingly richness of God love and favour. Her life after the encounter with Jesus was built on the decisions, she took on that day she met Jesus as the multitude throng and press him. She recognized that her defining moment is locked up in the actions she takes based on her decisions. She was unclean and an outcast abandoned by everyone due to the law.

She needed love, mercy, and a touch of compassion by Jesus Christ. So, in desperation she went through the crowd in faith and called out to

Jesus for mercy and healing. Like Bartimaeus she must have had heard of Jesus and his miracles, and learning that he was passing by, hoped to be delivered from the issue of blood for 12 years. She had an unshaken faith demonstrated by touching Jesus and would not be denied, although by law, she was not supposed to be in the mist of the crowd. She knew that was her moment of a lifetime.

The defining moment in her life came when in her demonstrated action, she did exactly what she has been saying privately to herself. Jesus knew someone had touched with strong faith different from the multitude. This is a lesson everyone that comes to Jesus must emulate, touch him by faith overcoming rejection and loneliness. We must receive from our Lord Jesus by a touch of faith and walk in the light of the word. This woman's story is the likewise of the defining moments of many believers all over the world because they, like her, have needed healing at some point or another and when they touched Jesus with their faith, their lives changed forever.

> "Therefore we also, since we are surrounded by so great a cloud of witnesses, let us lay aside every weight, and the sin which so easily ensnares us, and let us run with endurance the race that is set before us, [2] looking unto Jesus, the [a]author and finisher of our faith, who for the joy that was set before Him endured the cross, despising the shame, and has sat down at the right hand of the throne of God."

— HEBREWS 12:1-2

The woman had spent all her living upon physicians, but was not healed, When she came behind the Great Physician Jesus Christ, and touched the border of His garment: and immediately her issue of blood stanched. The love and grace of God gives you the opportunity that you can have a new beginning no matter what the mess up in your life. There are stories of many people with challenges and trials and seems to have made a failure of their lives, but the Devine intervention of God turned the situation around for wonderful testimonies to the glory of God

No individual can determine when the next defining moment will occur but there is something we can do and that is the decision to make the most of this very moment, today. There is great joy and wisdom in the decision to makes the most of every moment. When a child is born, parents do everything to capture every moment of their growth, but after a while they loose touch of this joy. The travail of life should not eliminate the wisdom making the most of every moment of life. Friends, my prayer for you today, is that the Holy Spirit will help you to walk in the wisdom taking daily the decision and action to make the most of every moment in life. Wisdom makes the most of every moment in life.

SEVEN

DETERMINATION

DETERMINE THAT YOU will let the Word of God not your past defines you. The healing of the man who was born blind demonstrates the truth that Jesus is the Light that brings light spiritually and physically to anyone willing to receive. Let the word of God define you and not your past. Therefore, if anyone is in Christ, he is a new creation; the old has gone, the new has come! that God was reconciling the world to himself in Christ, not counting men's sins against them.

> *"Then He who sat on the throne said, "Behold, I make all things new." And He said [a]to me, "Write, for these words are true and faithful." And He said to me, "It is done! I am the Alpha and the Omega, the Beginning, and the End. I will give of the fountain of the water of life freely to him who thirsts."*

— REVELATION 21:5-6

Be determined to take your eyes off your past failure, your inabilities and look up, See, I am doing a new thing! Now it springs up; do you not perceive it? I am making a way in the wilderness and streams in the wasteland. Old things must pass away, so take off the old temporary labels that once defined your life because of past mistakes, disappointment, and regrets, that is "less of me, more of Him," for this is a new day the Lord had made and rejoice because here comes your blessing.

The Lord Jesus Christ came to set us free from past failures and to give us hope, and when we focus on his love is what transforms our lives. What great compassion Jesus demonstrated to us by healing this man as an example for those that trust and have assurance of the love of God. The invitation from the heart of Love, proclaimed by this man who had a divine encounter with Jesus. The love of God is everlasting and will not fade away despite serious opposition from those who does not believe and have missed it. There is hope in Christ Jesus In the battle of life we encounter, because His presence is greater than rays of light breaking through the darkest night. Just as sure as the sun rises every morning, the presence of God breathes new hope and offers a fresh start every single day to every believer who waits on Him.

This man who was born blind expected to receive his sight and be free from blindness. The blindness became a past that cannot define him or prevent him from achieving his plans and purpose for life. When we need strength, direction healing and deliverance, we have a helper in the person of the holy Spirit, to accomplish by faith and receive the rich blessings of God's grace and mercy in the daily bread. God is love, full of compassion, and His mighty and faithful hands never fails to supply our needs according to His abundant supply.

According to the Scriptures the Lord is good. Let this define you that nothing can stop God from loving you and God is always good no matter what. The goodness of God never changes. This blind man when he discovered the abundant fruit from a life hidden in Christ is always gracious and loving, will not let go. He was full of determination and like a bulldog grabbing a bone and with holy boldness, he confronted the opposition. So, let God's love and grace define you, taking the moment to draw near to him daily, feeling His powerful presence surrounding you.

"As a father has compassion on his children, so the LORD
has compassion on those who fear him;"

— PSALMS 103:13

God is not offended by our weakness or imperfection. Our weakness
and difficult situations bring us on our knees before the almighty God
who is the lifter of our heads.

JESUS HEALS A MAN BORN BLIND

"Now as Jesus passed by, He saw a man who was blind from birth. And His disciples asked Him, saying, "Rabbi, who sinned, this man or his parents, that he was born blind?" Jesus answered, "Neither this man nor his parents sinned, but that the works of God should be revealed in him. I must work the works of Him who sent Me while it is day; the night is coming when no one can work. As long as I am in the world, I am the light of the world." When He had said these things, He spat on the ground and made clay with the saliva; and He anointed the eyes of the blind man with the clay. And He said to him, "Go, wash in the pool of Siloam" (which is translated, Sent). So, he went and washed, and came back seeing. Therefore, the neighbours and those who previously had seen that he was blind said, "Is not this he who sat and begged?" Some said, "This is he." Others said, "He is like him." He said, "I am he." Therefore, they said to him, "How were your eyes opened?" He answered and said, "A Man called Jesus made clay and anointed my eyes and said to me, 'Go to the pool of Siloam and wash.' So, I went and washed, and I received sight." Then they said to him, "Where is He?" He said, "I do not know."

— JOHN *9:1-12*

Jesus and His disciples see a man who was born blind, and the disciples ask him about the cause of the blindness. The disciples wanted to know if the blindness was a form of divine punishment for sin. The question is who sinned, this man or his parents, that he was born blind? That reveal that children could be impacted by the sin of their parents.

"you shall not bow down to them nor serve them. For I, the LORD your God, am a jealous God, visiting the iniquity of the fathers upon the children to the third and fourth generations of those who hate Me."

— EXODUS *20:5*

Jesus, clarified to the disciples that this case sin and punishment does not fit the case of congenital blindness. Moreover, Jesus did not explain what caused the blindness, but went on to explain to them what can be done about the blindness. *"Neither this man nor his parents sinned,"* said *Jesus, "but this happened so that the works of God might be displayed in him.* Jesus addresses the situation so that God's works will be done in it. The healing is fascinating because Jesus did not heal the man immediately but puts mud on the man's eyes and tells him to "go and wash" before he received his sight, and that's exactly what the man did.

THE PHARISEES EXCOMMUNICATE
THE HEALED MAN

"They brought him who formerly was blind to the Pharisees. Now it was a Sabbath when Jesus made the clay and opened his eyes. Then the Pharisees also asked him again how he had received his sight. He said to them, "He put clay on my eyes, and I washed, and I see." Therefore, some of the Pharisees said, "This Man is not from God, because He does not keep the Sabbath." Others said, "How can a man who is a sinner do such signs?" And there was a division among them. They said to the blind man again, "What do you say about Him because He opened your eyes?" He said, "He is a prophet." But the Jews did not believe concerning him, that he had been blind and received his sight, until they called the parents of him who had received his sight. And they asked them, saying, "Is this your son, who you say was born blind? How then does he now see?" His parents answered them and said, "We know that this is our son, and that he was born blind; but by what means he now sees we do not know, or who opened his eyes we do not know. He is of age; ask him. He will speak for himself." His parents said these things because they feared the Jews, for the Jews had agreed already that if anyone confessed that He was Christ, he would be put out of the synagogue. Therefore, his parents said, "He is of age; ask him." So, they again called the man who was blind, and said to him, "Give God the glory! We know that this Man is a sinner." He answered and said, "Whether He is a sinner or not I do not know. One thing I know: that though I was blind, now I see." Then they said to him again, "What did He do to you? How did He open your eyes?" He answered them, "I told you already, and you did not listen. Why do you want to hear it again? Do you also want to become His disciples?" Then they reviled him and said, "You are His disciple, but we are Moses' disciples. We know that God spoke to Moses; as for this fellow, we do not know where He is from." The man answered and said to them, "Why, this is a marvellous thing, that you do not know where He is from; yet He has opened my eyes! Now we know that God does not hear sinners; but if anyone is a worshiper of God and does His will, He hears him. Since the world began it has been unheard of that anyone opened the eyes of one who was born blind. If this Man were not from God, He could do nothing." They answered and said to him, "You were completely born in sins, and are you teaching us?" And they cast him out. True Vision and True Blindness Jesus heard that they had cast him out; and when He had found him, He said to him, "Do you believe in the Son of God?" He answered and said, "Who is He, Lord, that I may believe in Him?" And Jesus said to him, "You have both seen Him and it is He who is talking with you." Then he said, "Lord, I believe!" And he worshiped Him.

—JOHN 9:13-41

The testimony of this man will reveal that he became with unshaken and fearless determination a witness of Jesus whom he has never seen with his physical eyes. That makes the story especially fascinating to us today, we must be determined to bear witness of Jesus whom we have never seen with our physical eyes, except the eyes of faith. This is a defining moment that demonstrates who you are today and what you will become tomorrow. Wisdom, of a changed life is action, based on the grace of God, taking advantage and makes the most of every moment. Wisdom brings out the best in you. People of wisdom read, study and discipline themselves to achieve their set goals. They love what they do, and they do it with passion and determination. They learn from their past mistakes and from leaders in the specific area of interest. They are full of determination and never give up, even in the event of discouragement, opposition, and most especially they appreciate successes. They always keep on it, no matter how great the opposition or obstacles, going on and going on, until they accomplish all their set goals.

Are you self-motivated like this man born blind who received his sight? People like him, are self-motivating people who are aware of their past and use the breakthrough to thrive in the journey of life. They live joyfully and successfully in the present, always having a dream of a better future and a plan to achieve their set goals. They are not stagnant even in the event of rejection, but always with wisdom moving forward with bold strides.

The questions should be what are your life defining moments? Is there anything that led you to where you are? It could be that probably you cannot identify that defining moment, is there anything you need to do to make that happen? That defining moment is a point in your life when you're urged to make a pivotal decision. This could also be a moment you experience something that definitely changes the course of your life. These moments define you, and perfectly transforms your perceptions, behaviours, and life.

EIGHT
DILIGENCE

"Keep your heart with all diligence, For out of it spring the issues of life. Put away from you a deceitful mouth, And put perverse lips far from you. Let your eyes look straight ahead, And your eyelids look right before you. Ponder the path of your feet, And let all your ways be established."

— PROVERBS 4:23-26

YOUR HEART IS your most important area, not your knowledge, or abilities and it must be guarded diligently against deceptions, lies and others attacks of the power of darkness. Every person has a past, mistakes, disappointments, and probably regrets due to certain actions or words spoken to someone or even ourselves that we wish we had not, or it should not have happened. The people involved may have forgotten those incidents and may have dismissed them completely from their memories, but if you do not let go and forgive others and most importantly yourself, it will hinder growth and there is no success without personal growth. What defines you is not necessary the situations or circumstances but God's grace and your response or action to the exceedingly richness of God love and favour.

"Trust in the LORD with all your heart And lean not on your own understanding; In all your ways acknowledge Him, And He shall direct your paths."

— PROVERBS 3:5-6

Diligence can lead you to the define moment. Divine deposit is present in your life, but you must diligently discover your potential, strength and talents and focus your total power to use them to succeed in life. God uses people with failure and frustration in the past to perform signs and wonders through the life changing grace and wisdom of Him. When some people in the scripture stopped relying on that wisdom from above, disaster struck and lead to their downfall. Spiritual warfare or any kind of war is dangerous without the wisdom of God and any man or woman that attempts to build anything without wisdom is looking for trouble.

"the plans of the diligent lead surely to abundance, but everyone who is hasty comes only to want."

— PROVERBS 21:5

Wise planning requires making decisions for the long-term. It is dangerous to focus on your weakness or failures; rather, let them challenge you to bring out the overcomers in you. That is, by bringing out the best in you. Past failures should challenge you to always strive to do better because you are like a tree planted by streams of water; the fruit of success eventually comes if we keep working on it without giving up.

BE DILIGENT TO LEARN FROM PAST MISTAKES AND MOVE ON

"A slack hand causes poverty, but the hand of the diligent makes rich."

— PROVERBS 10:4

You must be diligent to acknowledge and correct past mistakes. Accept the necessary changes, implement them, and turn around completely. Let go past errors and resist the temptation of a lingering feeling of guilty conscience. Be ready to forgive others and most especially yourself for past mistakes, for lost opportunities, for not appreciating the opportunity that came your way. Diligently believe in your God given ability and talents, acknowledging the person you are, your present, having intensive excitement, passion, and a strong desire to achieve your goals and vision in the future. That comes from confident in your God given abilities and talents using to your advantage your past (either good or bad), your present and having courage that you can succeed in what you want to be in the future.

Whatever the level of your achievement and whatever state you find yourself, have confidence in your abilities, be diligent on the journey, and do not allow anybody to define you, because you are on a successful journey. Define your success and have peace, making the effort to diligently become the best that you can become. You must know your God ("Who is my God") spiritual identity, your family ("Who is my family") family tree and yourself ("Who am I") personal identity.

JOSEPH EXCELS IN DILIGENCE AND WAS BLESSED IN EVERY CIRCUMSTANCES

Genesis chapter 37 to 50 is the amazing story of the dreamer Joseph and the dysfunctional family of Jacob. His brothers hated him most especially in response to his dreams, which are revelations from God. A revelation which foretells a time when Joseph will rule over both his brothers and his parents. The brother's goal was to kill the dreamer and his dreams. God's grace and providence guided and protected Joseph's life, and instead he was sold into slavery and taken to Egypt. The deep pain caused by his brother's hatred, how very hard he must have plead for mercy and compassion from the sad rejection and cruelty. However, the scripture says, the Lord was with Joseph in every difficult moment. Joseph must have recalled with faith, in his heart many times about those covenant promises. I believe God was working on the life of Joseph and fulfilling those promises, by permitting him to go through those difficult circumstances and challenges.

At a very young age Joseph became a slave in Egypt. His slavery life is hardship, difficult and full of challenges. The brothers who should have protected and loved him sold him to Ishmaelite slave traders who brought him to Egypt, and there sold him to Potiphar an Egyptian. Potiphar as captain of the guard, working very close to the Pharaoh. meant that he had a high position in the Egyptian military, wealth, privilege, and prestige.

However, Potiphar's wife tries to seduce him, but he has the fear of God and respect for his master, so he is faithful in temptation. The past defining moments prepared him for the difficult circumstances, looking unto God for every moment of temptation. His various defining moments from the hatred of his brothers, moment of been thrown into pit and eventually the moment he was sold by his brothers, and finally the moment he became Potiphar's slave in a foreign land were used by God. All the various difficult defining moments were not wasted. They were all instruments that brought him closer to the Lord, and so he was prepared to look unto God for strength to overcome various challenges.

God never abandons us in difficult circumstances of our lives. God is always with us.

> "teaching them to observe all things that I have commanded you; and lo, I am with you always, even to the end of the age." Amen."

— MATTHEW 28:20

God was with Joseph, so His promise is that He is our strength and will never leave us nor forsake us. God was with Joseph, and he experienced the love and grace of God. The scriptures say Joseph was a prosperous man in the house of his master. A defining moment when he was made an overseer in the house of Potiphar, and over all that he had, and for Joseph's sake God blessed his house. God prospered him and through him brought a blessing to the house of his master. The blessing of the Lord was upon all that he had both in the house and in the field. Another defining moment was when Potiphar acknowledge that the Lord was with Joseph and that the Lord made all that he did to prosper in his hand. Potiphar also favoured Joseph because he was diligent, full of faith, and love the God of Israel. Joseph acquired more wisdom and abilities in management.

Diligence will bring out the best in you. The spiritual significance is that this story should inspire or motivate us to have passion coupled with diligence and a strong desire to always do our best whatever is the situation or circumstances. People of diligent obey God and discipline themselves to achieve their set goals. They have set goals and have a plan, and are doing their best to implement it. They act with passion and competence, learning from past mistakes and successes in their area of interest. They are full of determination and never give up, even in the event of partial failure, and most especially they celebrate successes. They diligently daily work on their plans until they become successful in achieving their set goals. They are self-motivating people who do not allow their past failures or success to hinder them in the journey of life. They live with joy in the present, keeping vision of a better future and a plan to achieve their set goals. They do not become stagnant in the event of a partial delay, but always moving forward with wisdom.

NINE

DISCIPLINE

DISCIPLINE YOURSELF TO let the Word of God not your past defines you. Take your eyes off your past failure, your inabilities and look up, God is doing a new thing! Now it springs up; do you not perceive it? God is making a way in the wilderness and streams in the wasteland. The scriptures reveal that the believer is dead to the old sin nature which was nailed to the cross with Jesus Christ. Therefore, also buried with Jesus, and just as He was raised up by the Father, so are believers raised up to "walk in newness of life. So having died with Christ, believers no longer live for themselves. Believers do not have to live in sin; they are now spiritually created in Christ.

> "Then He who sat on the throne said, "Behold, I make all things new." And He said to me, "Write, for these words are true and faithful." And He said to me, "It is done! I am the Alpha and the Omega, the Beginning, and the End. I will give of the fountain of the water of life freely to him who thirsts. He who overcomes shall inherit all things, and I will be his God and he shall be My son."

> — REVELATION 21:5-7

Therefore, if anyone is in Christ, he is a new creation; the old has gone, the new has come! that God was reconciling the world to himself in Christ, not counting men's sins against them. Always remember, to walk in the newness of life you must believe and act because old things must pass away, so take off the old temporary labels that once defined your life because of past mistakes, disappointments, and regrets, that is "less of me, more of Him," for this is a new day the Lord had made and rejoice because here comes your blessings.

JOSEPH REASSURES HIS BROTHERS

"When Joseph's brothers saw that their father was dead, they said, "Perhaps Joseph will hate us, and may actually repay us for all the evil which we did to him." So, they sent messengers to Joseph, saying, "Before your father died, he commanded, saying, 'Thus you shall say to Joseph: "I beg you, please forgive the trespass of your brothers and their sin; for they did evil to you."' Now, please, forgive the trespass of the servants of the God of your father." And Joseph wept when they spoke to him. Then his brothers also went and fell down before his face, and they said, "Behold, we are your servants." Joseph said to them, "Do not be afraid, for am I in the place of God? But as for you, you meant evil against me; but God meant it for good, in order to bring it about as it is this day, to save many people alive. Now therefore, do not be afraid; I will provide for you and your little ones." And he comforted them and spoke kindly to them."

— GENESIS 50:15-19

Discipline yourself to reflects upon your own traits, behaviours, and successes. A disciplined person has standards that enable him [or her] to match behaviour to beliefs. Take responsibility for your actions to build a strong character. There are moments that truly challenge us in a deeper way compelling us to choose between two solutions in which we strongly believe and are fully convinced. This I consider the epic of all Joseph's defining moments. This occurred in another very difficult moment in his life, after the death and burial of his father.

The brothers thought Joseph will take revenge of the evil they did to him, so they said, "Perhaps Joseph will hate us, and may actually repay us for all the evil which we did to him. So, they sent messengers to Joseph, saying, "Before your father died, he commanded, saying, 'Thus you shall say to Joseph: "I beg you, please forgive the trespass of your brothers and their sin; for they did evil to you.'" Now, please, forgive the trespass of the servants of the God of your father." Like Joseph our character is truly formed in defining moments because we commit to irreversible courses of action that share our formal and informal nature or personalities. These are moments of character revelations because our true nature is shown to everyone. In most cases these revelations are things that are new about us that are shown openly to others and even to ourselves.

They are moments of beam lights to expose something that had been hidden about our true nature. In some cases, we encounter a character test to prove or discover whether we will live up to our personal beliefs or hypocrisy. That why I consider this defining moment as the most challenging in the life of Joseph and some of us when we find ourselves in the position to forgive or "pay back" those you have rejected us, maltreated us, or hated us in the past. What do you do in these defining moments? Joseph wept and chose to act in love.

Joseph wept when they spoke to him and said to them, "Do not be afraid, for *am* I in the place of God? But as for you, you meant evil against me; *but* God meant it for good, in order to bring it about as *it is* this day, to save many people alive. Now therefore, do not be afraid; I will provide for you and your little ones." And he comforted them and spoke kindly to them. These are situations created by circumstance that demands action that reveals our true nature in Christ, because as He is, so are we in this world As confirmed in 1 John 4:17 (NKJV) "Love has been perfected among us in this: that we may have boldness in the day of judgment; because as He is, so are we in this world." We have to first recognize that the life we want tomorrow is built on the decisions we make today. We have to recognize that the defining moment is locked up in the actions we take based on our decisions.

Romans 12:18-19 says *Do not repay anyone evil for evil. Carefully consider what is right in the eyes of everybody. If it is possible on your part, live at peace with everyone. Do not avenge yourselves, beloved, but leave room for God's wrath. For it is written: "Vengeance is Mine; I will repay, says the Lord."*

The love and grace of God gives you the opportunity that you can have a new beginning no matter what the mess up in your life. Discipline yourself to become a man or woman of integrity and character. Defining moments like that of Joseph are critical and challenging with events that have mandatory options of choosing between two actions. In a dysfunctional family there are moments that could become more difficult to resolve. However, through discipline we can build our character to be men and women of integrity capable of doing what is right.

CONFESSION SECTION

7 DAYS DECREES TO DEFINE THE MOMENT

1. The love and grace of God gives you the opportunity that you can have a new beginning no matter what the mess up in your life.
2. We have to first recognize that the life we want tomorrow is built on the decisions we make today.
3. We have to recognize that the defining moment is locked up in the actions we take based on our decisions.
4. What defines you is not necessary the situations or circumstances but God's grace and our response or action to the exceedingly richness of God love and favour.
5. Discipline yourself to let the Word of God not your past defines you. Take your eyes off your past failure, your inabilities and look up, God is doing a new thing!
6. Defining moments like that of Joseph are critical and challenging with events that have mandatory options of choosing between two actions.
7. In a dysfunctional family there are moments that could become more difficult to resolve. However, through discipline we can build our character to be men and women of integrity capable of doing what is right.

THANK YOU!

I'd like to use this time to thank you for purchasing my books and helping my ministry and work.

You have already accomplished so much, but I would appreciate an honest review of some of my books on your favorite retailer. This is critical since reviews reflect how much an author's work is respected.

Please be aware that I read and value all comments and reviews. You can always post a review even though you haven't finished the book yet, and then edit your reviews later.

Thank you so much as you spare a precious moment of your time and may God bless you and meet you at the very point of your need.

Please send me an email at dr.pastormanny@gmail.com if you encounter any difficulty in leaving your review.

You can also send me an email at dr.pastormanny@gmail.com if you need prayers or counsel or you have questions. Better still if you want to be friends with me.

OTHER BOOKS BY EMMANUEL ATOE

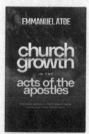

Church Growth in the Acts of the Apostles

The Church is the most powerful corporate body that is capable of commanding the attention of heaven on earth. The Church is God's idea and product, and so possesses an inbuilt capacity for success. The objective of this book is to get you acquainted with the purpose of the church in general, and the vision of Victory Sanctuary in particular.

A Moment of Prayer

There is nothing impossible with God but praying while breaking the law of God makes your prayers ineffective. Therefore, in this book, A Moment of Prayer, everyone under this program is expected to pray according to the rule, not against the law supporting it.

The Believer's Handbook

This book is highly recommendable for all. It is a book that will enhance your spiritual life, ignite the fire in you. It is a book that will open you heart to the mystery of faith.

The inestimable value of this book to every soul cannot be over emphasized. With this book you will get to know about the pillars of true faith in God. If you have been doubting your salvation, Christian life, the person and baptism of the Holy Ghost etc., this book is all you need.

Printed in the United States
by Baker & Taylor Publisher Services

Printed in the United States
by Baker & Taylor Publisher Services